BLOOMING BARE

MORGAN RICHARD OLIVIER

To the girl I was once was,
the woman I am,
and the queen I was created to be.

MORGAN RICHARD OLIVIER

TABLE OF CONTENTS

Introduction

Inked within these pages lies poetry and prose that embody the steppingstones of inner work, acceptance, and strength. They are the revelations, reflections, and reactions that we so commonly feel yet so rarely discuss. These are my words but our journeys.

The process of becoming B.A.R.E. requires us to identify our **brokenness**, **assess** ourselves fully, **redirect** our energies as a response to revelation, and **embrace** our truths, lessons, and testimonies. It is only after we remove the burdens that we can bloom boldly and unapologetically into the people that we were created to be.

———

There was season that awakened every emotion that lied dormant in my soul. A struggle that shook me to my core, broke my heart, and opened my eyes to an image of myself that externally was well put together yet internally falling apart. It was the realization that who I was and who I wanted to be weren't the same person. My plan had fallen apart and every aspect of my comfort fell with it.

My journey began with baggage I thought I needed to fly, but it only kept me grounded and going in circles.

In my insecurities I coasted on overcompensation, perfection, and people pleasing. In my iniquities I carried shame, regret, and anger. In my infuriation I bottled rage, strife, and bitterness that hurt me more than it could ever hurt anyone else. In my ignorance I held on to people, mindsets, and environments that were familiar but were leading me to failure and frustration.

Tired, tearful, and terrified it was clear that years of taking red flags and painting prettier pictures created a statue of myself that was molded by pain.

I so badly wanted to find my place in this world and in the hearts of the people who resonated in mine that I got lost along the way. I found burdens, bruising, and brokenness. Yet, in all of those, I found the awareness and meaning to push through my pain and see the bigger picture.

I now bear fruit because I healed myself from the root.

I am whole, protective of my peace, and brave enough to stand by my boundaries—embracing all that I am and all that I am not. It is in freedom that I flourish. Now, it's time for you to take the first step.

BLOOMING BARE

Blooming Bare

And after the tears had dried,
my vision and voice became clear.
From my darkest shadow pierced the purest light.
I found myself:
bruised, beautiful, and bare
stripped of every comfort
but clothed in truth.
Blooming where I was once broken.

BLOOMING BARE

MORGAN RICHARD OLIVIER

Breaking

Sometimes we get so wrapped up
in what others expect or want from us
that we lose sight
of what we want or need
to work on within ourselves.

Who were you—before the pain, the embarrassment, or
heartbreak? Who were you before your first experience that
popped in your head?

No matter what images come to mind, one thing is certain.
You are not and will never be the same.

The pain is
so hard to let go of
but so heavy to carry.

More to Life

There has to be more to life than this. Something greater than what lies in the midst of my comfort zone. Everything within me is telling me that there is something out there, but my eyes have yet to see what my gut so boldly wants me to know.

Having an *it's better than nothing* attitude
will lead you to settle for just about anything.

What Matters Most

It's so easy to get wrapped up in the opinions of others, whenever you haven't quite identified or found love in the person that you are. You drain yourself by trying to measure up to expectations or find yourself crushed defending your truth whenever it seems you are surrounded by lies. But you must never forget one simple truth. No one's feelings about you should ever overpower the facts of who you are. You can't control the words, beliefs, or actions of others but you can control your own. It's not about the world liking you. It's about knowing, understanding, and loving yourself.

Depth Desired

Some people desire attention, money, and gifts. I personally crave depth, comprehension, and learning.

Teach me something. Tell me about your life experiences and the lessons you've learned. Discuss psychology and your spiritual journey. Give me depth and authenticity. I'd rather empathize and have thought provoking conversations with a small group than feel alone and bombarded by the energy of large crowds that have nothing authentic or productive to offer.

Sometimes I feel like I'm drowning in depression because I'm trying to be understood by a shallow world.

I wanted so badly to fit in,
but the more included I was
the lonelier I felt.

This Too Shall Pass

Life—though beautiful—can sometimes feel like an unpredictable disaster. There are days we feel like the whole world is that our fingertips while other days it feels as though the weight of the world is on our shoulders.

For so many of us, behind our beautiful smiles is the burden of an internal struggle. Behind the cute photos of the baby you prayed for, you may be suffering with postpartum depression. Behind the titles and accomplishments, there may be emptiness and insecurities. Behind what appears to be the perfect life may be a person struggling with past traumas, current struggles, and thoughts of suicide. Whatever it may be, I want you to know and truly understand that you are never alone. If you ever feel like you can't hold on anymore, please reach out to someone that can help you carry your cross. Seek help and remember that these troubles are temporary. You can and will overcome all that you're facing. Give yourself all of the time, patience, and compassion that you need.

Destroy the idea of perfection
before it destroys you.

Media Muse

Can't you see it?
I'm dying inside.
Rattled with anger,
Poisoned from pride.
There's a caged animal screaming
Behind these innocent eyes.
To the world I'm always laughing
But alone all I do is cry.
For far too long
Social media has been my stage.
I'll compartmentalize my loneliness
If you like and follow my page.
The world sees a perfect queen
But in the mirror I see a clown.
Let's see who still loves me
When I put the mask down.

Be Kind Always

No amount of money, make up, or materials could ever cover up that fact that we are all human. However, we often forget that behind social media facades there are many people that are struggling daily. We all roam this Earth with concerns, conditions, and circumstances of our own. Sometimes you'd never suspect that the strong person next to you is crying themselves to sleep every night. You don't know if the person that's trying to encourage everyone has thought about taking their life. You don't know if the person that is smiling and laughing in your face is slowly losing their battle with depression behind closed doors. You never know what someone else is going through, but you do know that being a kind person goes a long way.

The Illusion of Emptiness

So often, the world is fooled by numbers. Spectators believe that the number of friends in your photos reflect how likable you are. They think the amount of square feet in your home is a testament to your financial success. They believe the amount of money and items you possess are a reflection of your influence. They think that by having a lot you long for little.

The thing about emptiness is that it doesn't care about numbers. It doesn't care about the stage of life you're currently in or your age. It doesn't care if you have money, cars, children, a marriage, or all of the degrees in the world.

That is because emptiness is a state of mind. No tangible thing can fill it.

You don't truly know
the depth of your pain
until you are pleading
and crying out to God for help.

When nothing makes sense
and all that was once clear
is clouded with doubt,
you begin to realize
just how fragile you are.

No one has hurt me
quite like I've hurt myself.

Sometimes it seems like a curse to empathize so intensely.
It is my most beautiful strength yet ugliest weakness
to identify the pain of others while deeply feeling it within
myself. That internal need to heal everyone's ails has led me to
create my own.

My distance is not
meant to hurt you.
It's to protect
myself.

Don't Let Go

I see you. Clinging to what's left of your hope, looking for any sign to keep going, and questioning every aspect of your existence. It's a place many of us are familiar with but no one likes to talk about. Truth is, behind that youth is an old pain that wakes you up every morning and rocks you to sleep at night. My tired love, I need you to understand that there is more than this suffering and struggle. There is far more for you than what you feel, think, and know. You don't want to die. You want the pain to die, the fear to subside, and peace to embrace you more than emptiness has. You want this season to end, not your life. No matter how hard it gets, lonely it seems, and difficult it becomes to navigate—you cannot stop. No matter what is overwhelming you, you will overcome.

I got lost in the world
trying to find the very things
that were already within me.

Projection is toxic to everyone involved.
Instead of taking your pain out on those around you,
take multiple steps back and try to identify the source
of the pain within you.

Why

Sometimes we trust the wrong people, find ourselves surrounded by fake friends, place our hearts in the wrong hands, and feel lost amongst those we once held in high regard. We can be mad all day, blame them for our problems, and even throw a pity party about how things panned out—but if we really want to learn and grow then we must take some accountability.
We allowed these problems and people into our lives.

They key is understanding why.

I tried so hard
for you to recognize my worth
because I truly didn't know
what it was.

BLOOMING BARE

Coming to terms with your place
in someone's life
can be difficult.

What's sometimes even harder
is accepting that they may no longer
have a place in yours.

In trying to fix you
I have broken myself.
In trying to be what was expected of me
I have alienated every ounce of authenticity.

I simply can't do it anymore:
the perfection, the sadness, the unattainable goals.
Maybe this breaking is meant to bring me together:
truly, honestly, and unapologetically.

Release Without Reconnection

We will all face experiences that shake us to the core. Whether it's heartbreak, betrayal, or unsettling circumstances—we will experience a hurt that we expect another person to repair as if they need to admit their wrongs and apologize for us to move forward.

The problem is that we waste our time and tears on the response of people that hurt us in the first place. We think that if they tell us sorry that the wound will be healed. And although that may work for some, others must accept that the apology may never come. That person may never even see a need to be sorry—even if you break down the reason as to why they should.

Don't base your healing on another person's words or reactions. Seek healing within yourself, forgive that person, and move forward knowing that you learned and grew from it all. It doesn't make what they did okay—but waiting for healing from those that bring hurt isn't okay either.

The Detour

It was darkness that made you seek the light and going off course that helped you align with a greater path. The detour always had a deeper meaning. It's losing the desire to control every aspect of your current circumstances that helps you gain confidence in what is to be.

It's your lack of healing
that is hindering you.

It's my love for potential
that causes me pain.
The desire to push people
to become better with time
always has a way of making
me waste my own.

When the Cup Runs Dry

Sometimes the people you would give your life for will not care
about you. Sometimes the people you openly defend in public
are the same ones trying to destroy your character in private. It's
a difficult truth but one that opens your eyes to one of the realest
lessons you will come to learn. You don't always get what you
give.

You can't create chaos
in the lives of others
and expect peace
to come to yours.

No matter what they did
or how you feel,
causing hurt to others
will never bring healing to you.

BLOOMING BARE

It's out of my hands
but not out of my mind.

Silent Reading

Everyone has a chapter of their life they'd rather not read out loud, times and testimonies they share humbly with an appropriate few, and a wisdom that only stems from a fool's experience. As tempted as we are to let those pages define or derail us, we have to remember that our story does not end there. If we repented, learned, and grew from that chapter—that's where many of our spiritual journeys began. Not a single page was a surprise to God. He used our broken pieces to not only get our attention but also to create something even more beautiful. Turn the page, keep going, and find peace in knowing that it's your plot twist that aligned you with purpose. Your story is far from over, and there is no better time to revise it than now.

After wasting so much time worrying about the irrelevant opinions of irrelevant people, it became clear that the person whose respect, love, and acceptance I valued most was me. I owed it to myself to dig deeper, forgive fully, and identify beauty that had been hidden beneath burdens for so long.

Sometimes the hardest truth to accept
is that no amount of love or effort
can change people that don't work
toward changing themselves.

There's a love and pain that I've become familiar with that has changed faces throughout my life. This was a love that once caused me to pour every ounce of energy into "the good" of other people—yet it left me with nothing for myself. And after tears and acceptance, it became clear that boundaries, prayer, and closure had to fill a space where every ounce of hope once was.

Sometimes you have to distance yourself
to get a clearer picture
of what's happening around you.

Whenever I stopped making excuses
for my unacceptable behavior,
I stopped accepting it
from others as well.

Cordial > Close

I've reached a point where I'm tired of being hurt
by people that I allow into my life.
I've learned that the cut is deeper when the bond is tighter,
and bitterness can find itself seeping into places
where unmatched loyalty once resided.

Therefore, I would rather be cordial with people than be close.
I'd rather pray for you and love you from afar
than have you in my life
and feel your loyalty to me is miles away.

You don't need an apology
to gain closure.

Seek healing,
find forgiveness,
and move on.

Bringing others down
will never lift you out
of your own pit
or solve your problems.

I've Washed My Hands of You

I do not have the time, energy, or desire to be anyone's enemy. If you've hurt me in any way, just know that I have no intent to hurt you back. I will not attack your character, tell lies about you, or worse—tell the truth. I will simply carry on and allow you to do the same, knowing that God will handle you in His time and in ways that are far greater than I ever could.

If I'm angry, there is still hope.

As long as there are tears, words, and concern—there is care.

But once I become silent,
my efforts become nonexistent
and so does your place in my life.

They don't need to know
your side of the story,
and you don't need
the last word.

Seek healing
and you'll find peace
in not proving
your point.

Mask Off

In the end, people always have a way
of revealing who they are.
You just have to give them
the space and time to do so.

No mask can be worn forever.

It's not that you don't want love.
The truth is that you don't want the pain.
You fear the possibility of rejection
and the idea of being broken again,
after you've worked so hard to piece yourself
back together.

It was accepting my part in the pain
I allowed in my life
that made the difference.

You've let me down
more times than I'll ever allow
myself to pick you up.

Dig Deep

Until you are happy with yourself, everyone will always look better. Until you love yourself truly, you will always give more love and energy to people that don't deserve it. Sometimes you have to ignore those thoughts in your mind because they are just that…thoughts. You are much more than you give yourself credit for. Put your energy into yourself and you'll see that what you're looking for in the world is already inside of you.

The biggest mistake you'll ever make
and the most haunting regret you'll ever have
is knowing that you didn't even try.

The objective is never
to hurt someone back.
It's to heal yourself.

Misery should not
seek company.
It should seek
its source.

Why is it so common
that we love others
to the point that
we end up hating
ourselves?

Funny how we see the potential
in people that may not exist
yet fail to identify the power
within ourselves.

If I Could Hurt You

If I had the chance to hurt you like you hurt the world, I wouldn't. I wouldn't summon your love for my pleasure alone. I wouldn't try to tarnish your reputation to boost my ego. I wouldn't make your vulnerability my source of entertainment. I wouldn't abuse your friendship to get what I want. I wouldn't blindside you with the burdens you brought me.

Instead, I would open your eyes and impact your mind. I would break you down to the foundation so that I could build you back up. Not to bring you misery, but to show you meaning—to alter your motives and purify your mind. I would change your perspective and heal the parts of you that want to hurt people because you are truly hurt yourself.

Meaning Matters

Sometimes we desire
so deeply
to be wanted
that we forget
the importance
of being truly
valued and appreciated.

Insecurity will have you
going out of your way
to hurt the very people
that were sent to help you.

Attached to Acceptance

I wish I could say it didn't faze me. I would be lying if I said it didn't hurt. Truth is, I cried many nights and lost hours of sleep over it all. I felt betrayed and foolish, but not simply because you showed your true colors beyond recognition. It's because for years I saw the signs and refused to let you go. I took your true colors, painted prettier pictures, and enabled and made excuses for you along the way. I refused to believe that someone I loved and protected to no end would turn on me in a way that not only insulted my intelligence but also took advantage of the love and loyalty I always showed. For that, I wasn't mad at you. I was disappointed in myself. Because you never valued my presence or truly loved me. You were merely an attachment. You loved the idea of me, and I loved the acceptance from you.

Still I try to fix you,
as I cut myself on every one
of your broken pieces.

It's your actions
not aligning
with my expectations
that hurt me most.

If you'd hurt me, it would help.
It would make every step more freeing
to walk away.

Because holding on to you
is destroying every shred of peace
in my life.

But the thought of releasing you
is more painful than words
can describe.

We make time for people and things
that mean something to us.

If someone loves you,
they will give you their effort
—not their excuses.

It Hurts to Help

Sometimes in trying to help others, we hurt ourselves.
We fail to distinguish the difference between assisting and
enabling, as we try with everything in us to bring out the best in
people.

Unfortunately, the only people that are capable of change
are the ones who truly want it. The ones who work for it.
The ones who aspire to be healed.

You pushed me away
and I decided it wasn't
worth the journey back.

MORGAN RICHARD OLIVIER

I held on
to the point
I let myself go.

BLOOMING BARE

I've grown tired
of giving my strength to weak people
and crying over what
no longer makes me smile.

/

Stop letting people
that add so little to your life
take so much of your peace.

Your Audience

To the person who has gone through hell and back dealing with the schemes of their enemies. Allow me to make something very clear. People can do many things, but they can never take your talents, your truth, or anything God has for you.

The thing about weak and destructive people is that they truly believe that they have the authority or ability to destroy others. Whenever they're in a season where their attacks are notably affecting people, they experience a high. Your struggling brings them happiness. However, you and I both know that though you may fall, it is only a matter of time before you get back up. And that is when the hating truly begins.

The ones that like you the least watch you the most.

So, what do you do? Nothing. Let them watch, let them hate, and let them go. Allow them to learn this lesson of their weak projection as their actions taught you the power of protecting your peace.

Because, at the end of the day, people that truly love and honor themselves don't have time to worry about anyone that isn't with or for them. Their past enemies are their present inspiration.

Empathy for Enemies

I don't wish them harm. I wish they could feel what I once felt. I wish they could feel the rejection their betrayal left me with. I wish they could feel the true sorrow I felt for hurting them. I wish they could feel the immeasurable love and loyalty in my heart I once had for them. I wish they could feel the sadness and suffering they caused me to endure.

Because the true measure of my pain would not be exchanged in evil but only understood through empathy.

Be Still

How many nights have you cried yourself to sleep worrying about the insensitive, inaccurate, or ignorant things people have said or thought about you? How many months have walked around with the weight of the world on your shoulders because you are so angry or hurt about how a situation played out? How many years of your life have you wasted trying to prove your value to people that refuse to recognize your worth?

Understand me whenever I say that this needs to be the moment that you stop. No matter who it was, what it was, or even why—you have to detach before it destroys you.

Having the last word or holding a grudge will not help you seek healing or closure. It will not right a wrong, and it will only hurt you more in the end. Sometimes you have to shut your mouth and open your eyes to what God is revealing within you and around you. Be still.

People may judge, talk, and even misinterpret your actions (or lack of reaction) and that's fine. It's not about that. It's not about being understood, getting even, or having anyone see your side. It's about your overall wellbeing, character, and alignment.

Tears to Triumph

I remember the days I cried because I was actually waking up in the morning and the nights I couldn't sleep because my anxiety and depression weighed so heavily on me. I remember feeling like I had no idea what I was doing with my life. More importantly, I remember actively and honestly doing something about it.

Working on my mental and spiritual health was not some walk in the park. It was difficult, eye-opening, and at times a painfully lonely walk. However, with each step, I grew stronger and wiser. I not only learned from my emotions and experiences, but I also learned *why* I felt them in the first place.

Don't give up on your journey because this chapter is hard. Search yourself, seek God, and heal from all that is hurting you. This season is not meant to destroy you. It is here to develop you.

Purpose Perspective

It's tempting to get caught up in the emotions of our experiences. We feel overtaken by the wrongs we've done or wrongs that have been done to us. Even when we feel we are moving forward, the progress is short lived because we always revert back to the pain, shame, or anger.

It doesn't have to be that way. If we choose to see each experience as a lesson, we will see that all pain has worked and can work as an opportunity to grow.

Choose to see how much you've grown from that point. Understand that wisdom often comes from experience and that everything from the past was needed for you to become the person that you are today. Stop giving your power to pain. Let the pain propel you.

Life Saver

I used to be a person who struggled with regret, rejection, and the inability to release pain until I realized that pain is sometimes the language that God speaks to me in—and it's a language I listen to very well.

Pain is oftentimes what gets our attention. The loss of a loved one shows us the importance of appreciating our family, true friends, and life. The consequences that arise from foolish actions and experiences—if we choose to learn from them—can leave us with a greater understanding and wisdom. The people who attack our character or seemingly jump through every hoop to destroy us teach us the importance of knowing ourselves and remind us that we never want to be that weak.

My pain bolstered my empathy, endurance, and enlightenment. Because of that, I see every struggle as a blessing in disguise. My pain didn't stop me. It's what got me started.

The Plan

You are never alone. You are never so broken that you can't be put back together again. You may feel lost, but God sees and knows exactly where you are. There is a greater purpose for every single pain, problem, and even promotion that was allowed into your life. He has a plan, even when you feel all of your plans have failed.

So, I started at rock bottom,
in the still darkness,
where my tears saturated the ground
and in the very mud my name was dragged through.

With my hands shaking but sure,
I picked the seeds of my struggles
and aligned them with lessons
in hope that they could be cured and cultivated
to create something new.

It was a time for planting
and a season I knew my pain and pressure
served a much greater purpose.

With time, intention, and tending
something beautiful could blossom
in a place that was bound for so long.

BLOOMING BARE

Assessing

It's the silent truths
that speak volumes.

You can't heal from a hurt
that you're trying to hide.

I've grown tired
of fighting to hold on
to all that I've outgrown.
Most of all,
I'm tired of fighting myself.

Mirror Mirror

At some point, you must consider the possibility that you are the problem. That maybe the reason why things aren't working out for you or why people are detaching from you is because of a flaw in your character or your perspective on life. It's not negative self-talk—it's an assessment of yourself. You can't blame the world around you for everything and expect anything to change for you or within you. Check yourself and your progress often.

Often the person who's hurting your growth and relationships most is the one in the mirror.

Until we address what's within,
we will always feel that we are without.

Responsibility

No one is responsible for your health, healing, or happiness but you. You can blame your exes, enemies, parents, spouse, children, friends, employers and everyone else under the sun. However, until you understand that you are responsible for your own life, all that you are facing will remain the same.

You are the one who needs to take responsibility for your life and the direction you want your life to go. The world is not going to hand you happiness, healing, or health on a silver platter. Through your choices, thoughts, and beliefs you will create it for yourself.

People can't give you
what they don't have.
It is up to you to obtain and observe
all that is needed
for your growth, peace, and progress.

Be the Change

If we want to change our lives, then we must change ourselves. Comparing, complaining, and projecting will do nothing for our overall progress. We must hold ourselves accountable and actively work on our mental, physical, and spiritual health. We have to make the change if we want to see a change.

Take the Steps

I know at times it was overwhelming and caused you many tears. I understand it was uncomfortable and made you wonder if it was best to stay as you were. But as each step begins to get a little easier and those fingers slowly release the grip of the weights you've been carrying, you should know and always remember this profound truth. You did the right thing.

Detaching from a mindset, person, trauma, pain, or lifestyle is far more than giving up on someone or something. It's picking yourself up and finally realizing the importance of aligning yourself with better.

Give yourself time to adjust to your journey. Be patient as your emotions and environments evolve. Be proud of the strides you made and the joys that are to come. There is peace in knowing that God has a plan and knows exactly where you are right now. You've made room for greater and in due time you will get there.

MORGAN RICHARD OLIVIER

Maybe God's not changing your situation
because He's trying to change you.

Remember Your Name

It's easy to get engulfed in the storms of life and even easier to stay mentally shackled to them. Even when our circumstances change, we manage to stay condemned and crushed due to our own mental prison or because we're being judged by the court of public opinion. Lucky for us, how we feel doesn't dictate our fate.

We can't lose sight of the fact that our journey isn't intended to end there. No matter how it feels or what others think, we are better than that.

Regardless of what's said, done, or thrown at you it's important to never forget who you truly are. It's critical that you remember that you are not defined by any experience, person, problem, or pain.

Whenever the weak try to call you down by your fears, failures, and shortcomings, remember that the only people that can pull you down are the ones beneath you.

Long before you had an insecurity and others had an opinion, God gave you a name and a purpose.

Rise Above

Sometimes we find ourselves bogged down by the pressures, problems, and pains of this world and only become more drained whenever we try to carry, address, or express them. This is because some things aren't worth the fight, energy, and entertainment. We must discern the mindsets, people, situations, and insecurities that are pure distractions sent to lead us off course, traveling in circles, and stuck in a rut. The only way to overcome some obstacles is to rise above them.

There is always a lesson to be learned but first we have to get up and see the bigger picture. Whenever we take ourselves out of the place of emotion, lift our spirits, and re-examine ourselves and issues from an elevated place of humility and growth, we see that what once seemed too big to overcome was simply a steppingstone to equip us for something greater. Sometimes God doesn't allow our reality to change until we learn and grow from it. Our outlook, direction, and life changes whenever we do.

Stay the Course

Whenever you reach the point of exhaustion and feel like it's easier to just give up on your goals, faith, or progression—I want you to remember this one thing. Walking away from a path that was purposed for you will not only make the journey harder, but can also cause you to walk in regret, sadness, and confusion.

Don't stop. Seek discernment and determine when it's time to rest and when it's time to release.

I encourage you to walk away from the fears that seem to paralyze you, the doubts that are draining you, and all the burdens you've been carrying thus far.

No matter how slow, trying, or difficult each step may be—they are still steps in the right direction and will be well worth it in due time. Never stop moving forward. Something greater is waiting.

Their feelings do not
outweigh the facts
about who you are

Bigger

Before you waste another moment of your life worrying about the opinions of others, the expectations of those around you, or the box your community may expect you to fit in—remember one thing. The world is a big place, and you dictate your place in it.

There are people that are throwing their potential and passions away because they aren't understood by those around them. They are throwing their powerful futures away because someone is always trying to keep them bound by their imperfect pasts.

You can't do this.

Don't let small minds or small towns lead you to limit your dreams, make you feel stuck in their idea of you, or cause you to believe that what you see is all that is out there. There is more to you and more for you. Take a step out of your comfort zone and understand that what God has and means for you has the power to impact the world. Don't hide your talents, experiences, strengths, views, or creativity due to the fear of what a few may think. The world needs what you have. It's time to share it.

Heal

Your healing is about more than your current discomfort or wanting to get back to normal. Healing is a physical, mental, spiritual, and emotional release of what is keeping you bound. The process will not be understood by everyone and at times it may not even make sense to you. However, you must understand that your healing today (or lack of) sets the tone for your tomorrows and the future of your children.

Heal and deal from within.
Take as much time as you need.
Embark on the journey of healing
without explanation, excuse, and an audience.

Heal so that your next generation will not be bound by whatever broke you.

The people that hurt you
should not dictate the way
in which you heal.

Refrain

Often the best thing you can do is pray about it, leave it alone, stay silent, and lay low as you let God do His thing. The timeline may not be what you want, but I promise that in due time it will work in your favor.

If we are more concerned
about the problems and mess
of other people's lives,
we are not actively and honestly
working on our own.

If only we could undo the pain of the past
but keep the wisdom from the lessons.

Solitude

It was in isolation
That I realized that solitude did not mean lonely.
The darkness was not there to overtake me.
It came to enlighten me
To get my attention and focus on what truly brought me light.
It started out uncomfortable
But in the end, brought a new meaning of peace.
Solitude is nothing to fear.
It is freedom.

MORGAN RICHARD OLIVIER

I've come to accept the fact
that although I live to understand,
I may never be understood.

Impact > Impress

We live in a society that idolizes fake love, fake success, and fake happiness yet we turn away from conversations about real personal struggles, real world issues, and real perseverance. We'll never truly impact others until we get over the destructive desire to impress them.

It isn't a matter of you being weak.
It's the issue of you giving your power, love, and energy to the
wrong thoughts, people, and things. Give yourself the love,
compassion, and strength that you selflessly offer to the world.

No Rain, No Flowers

There were times in my life where I was lost, a loner, and a fool.

Days where I drowned in self-loathing and wondered if I'd ever be able to keep my head above water. Nights where I questioned how it was humanly possible to produce so many tears.

As tempting as it once was to look back at those times with bitterness, I can't help but see all the blessings and beauty that came from brokenness. It's in those times that I learned the most and gained the empathy and endurance that I have today. It's those times that taught me to let go of my ego and focus on my emotional health and eternity.

Trust me whenever I tell you that all things are working together for your good. That includes the bad times, the hard times, and even the times that make you question if you're going to make it through. God has a purpose for your pain, your past, and even your imperfections. It's all part of a greater plan and will be used for His glory whenever you make the choice to learn and grow from it.

So, shake off the shame, and embrace all the wisdom that those storms showered you with. Like all of God's beautiful creations, in due time the rain will help you grow.

The likes and approval
from the world
mean absolutely nothing
if you don't first love yourself
from within.

Don't be so busy trying to
convince others of your happiness
that you make yourself miserable.

Replaced

How are we that easily replaced when we were always there? Do they not recall how we gave, loved, and supported them when they couldn't seem to extend it to themselves? How could we remember these times so vividly, and yet their actions would lead us to believe that they forgot?

It's simple.

They don't remember when the need has been fulfilled. They won't miss you whenever you're gone. They will miss you whenever that person or thing they replaced you with is no longer accessible.

How do you expect to change your life
if you refuse to change your routine or mindset?

What Really Matters

Compliments may put a smile on your face and having a group of people clapping for you may feel empowering. However, there is no amount of outside validation that can heal or enhance your soul. Search yourself, identify and address your voids, and then fill them with the forgiveness, love, and understanding that you truly deserve.

Validation may satisfy your ego
but it will never soothe your soul.

MORGAN RICHARD OLIVIER

You don't need more people to communicate with.
You need people that can truly comprehend you.
Those who understand where you're coming from
and want to help you reach where you want to go.

My silence speaks volumes
and my absence will let you know
exactly where I stand.

I'm not one to respond or react to fools.
I remove myself from them.

Don't let any person, social media account, or emotion
push you in a direction that can destroy you.
Seek discernment and let God order the steps
to your ultimate destination.

Funny how people
will view you as a liar
until they start
living your truth.

The hurt aren't healing and
the healed aren't hurting

Being strong
doesn't mean
you have to
suffer in silence.

Energy Allocation

One of the main reasons why we feel drained, worried, or stagnant in life is not because we lack strength, ability, or the desire to be better. It's because we deplete our efforts on things we shouldn't entertain.

Fast or Feed

Whatever we feed will grow. Therefore, if we feed our focus on people, problems, or places that bear no fruit, we are not only wasting time but also wasting the ability to bear our own. Focus on what and who truly matters. Make the decision to put progression over people-pleasing and inward assessment over outside validation. You have the power to make a positive difference in your life and lives of others, but first you have to make your mindset and movements a priority.

Protect Your Peace

Peace came when I removed the impulse to respond to petty people and things. Once I realized that the weakest people desired my strongest responses—that's when I discovered the power of detachment and distance.

I did not have the energy or aspiration to put people in their place, after I came to terms with the fact that I no longer wanted them to have a place in my life. I was too old to correct childish behavior and found it pointless seeing that I didn't have children of my own. It was identifying and accepting the fact that not everyone is worthy of my words and even fewer deserved my presence that aligned me with a greater level of peace and order.

I encourage you to take your power back and remember that you determine who and what gets your energy and attention. No one is owed access to you, and there is no need for explanation. Protect your peace, heal your pain, and stay focused on what and who matters. Stop reacting and giving responses in areas of your life that need to be removed.

Stop making room for people
that don't value their place in your life.

Be careful who you open up to.
Some want a testimony,
others just want tea.

Learn to pray about your problems
more than you vent about them.

Empty Figures

Do not let this shallow world fool you.
There are people with all the money in the world
who harbor the poorest spirits.
Influential figures with the best reputations
and no moral character.

MORGAN RICHARD OLIVIER

Before putting someone in their place,
make sure you're in yours.

BLOOMING BARE

Often our feeling of lack and emptiness
stems from our inability to identify and protect
all that we should be grateful for.

Our desire for more
leads us to appreciate less,
and the pressure to fill our voids
only creates more.

If you don't control your emotions
your emotions will find a way to control you.

Not everything and everyone
deserves your energy.

Allowing yourself to be vulnerable
is a strength in itself,
but vulnerability without discernment
is dangerous.

And then I realized
the fire was always burning
within me,
but the flames were busy
keeping everyone else warm.

Words are meaningless
if our movements
don't match
our message.

Faith and Fixing

So often we want to fix others and make them better. We want to give them all of the tools to succeed, see past their red flags, and carry their slack until they get it together. Maybe it's because we see a little bit of our past selves in them. As empathic and kindhearted as we may be, we have to remember that for us to grow we had to put in the work. We had to want to be better and make the choices and sacrifices to reach our healing.

We can love, support, and encourage people but we alone cannot fix them.

I'm just an old soul
with naive eyes
trying to make sense
of the world around me.

The ability to identify your own toxicity
is not only a sign of strength
but also an indication of maturity.

Blameless and Shameless

Anyone can blame the world, project their issues upon everyone they know, and live a life of selfishness. However, it takes strength, maturity, and humility to identify and address our own weaknesses, shortcomings, and toxic traits.

Wait for It

Just because you don't accomplish, receive, or see something in the time frame that you want—it doesn't mean that you've failed or missed your mark. It doesn't mean that it's too late. What's meant and aligned for you will come at the right time. It will come at a time that you are truly ready to handle, appreciate, and understand it. Don't let your worry overshadow the work.

Divine Disruption

As I look back over what I thought was a season of destruction, I now see God's clear plan of development. Nothing that was ruined was meant to be restored. I needed the revelation of my own toxic traits and expired relationships so that I could be redirected to redemption and restoration.

Embrace but Exit Isolation

Isolation—though oftentimes misunderstood—is beautiful.
It's a place where you can lose the world and find yourself.
A season in life where you not only identify and face your
demons, but also discover what they've been feeding on for so
long.

And although isolation may be safe and secure, we must face the
fact that it is not meant to stay. We must not only face ourselves
but also face the world again.

It's okay if you're nervous at first—unsure if people will accept
or comprehend the new enlightened you. It may take them a
while or it may never come at all, but one thing is sure. You
can't and don't ever want to go back to the way things were. So,
don't! Revel in your truth, embrace the journey you've grown
on, walk in your wisdom, and accept all of the blessings that lie
ahead of you. Don't let your comfort cripple you. Welcome and
be the light.

BLOOMING BARE

MORGAN RICHARD OLIVIER

Redirecting

Leave it behind

The person,
the mindset,
the environment
that is dragging you down.

The Difference

The person you were, the person you currently are, and the person you were created to be are three different people.

Some of us are rising but are scared to truly shine because we do not have confidence in our authority, or we fear that others do not see us for who we've become. However, truth of the matter is that our authenticity and assignment is much more important than outside approval or internal acceptance.

Not everyone will understand or respect the power of repentance, redemption, enlightenment, refinement, or transformation. Ascend, move forward, and prune anyway. We may experience fear, discomfort, and question the promise and instructions God gave us. Be obedient, endure, and trust the process anyway. It's less about who we or others think we are. It's about remembering and knowing to whom we belong.

People will try to remind you of where you've been,
whenever they are intimidated by where you're going.

Envision Exodus

One of the hardest lessons I've learned—and one that took so long to understand—is that God will deliver you, redeem you, and define you but still allow your storms and enemies to carry on.

You will be saved, growing, learning, and becoming closer to God as each day passes, *yet* it will seem like every time you look over shoulder you will see those seeking to destroy, defame, and distract you.

That is not because God is blind to your efforts, ignoring your prayers, or has forgotten you. Everything is allowed because it is part of His strategy.

Always remember that the same God that created the sea is the same God that suddenly parted it to set the captives free. Only when He saw His people were across, safe, and ready did He turn the tide to drown their enemies and block their way of returning to a place of destruction.

Stay focused, continue planting good seeds, keep moving forward, and do not be fooled by people and things committed to keeping you bound. God's going to take care of them. Press on to your breakthrough, and don't look back. This isn't your season of entertaining. This is your Exodus. Focus on your faith. You're coming out.

Outdated and Outgrown

Sometimes it's the foolish desire to be close to people that are no longer suitable for our growth that prevents us from growing in areas and relationships that were destined to help us reach our destination.

Growing Pains

I'm either growing with you or I'm outgrowing you. Either way, I'm leveling up.

I used to fear not being accepted or understood. Now, I fear falling out of alignment or living a mediocre life. That's because as my awareness and call to purpose grew so did my goals and standards. I realized that if I wanted to be more, I needed to stop settling for less. Growth, as beautiful as it may be, can be a very lonely and eye-opening process. A journey that teaches us that sometimes to get to our destination, we will have to take necessary steps alone.

If it doesn't help you grow, you need to let it go.
As difficult as it may be to release people, mindsets, and environments that are familiar to you—I promise the burden is much heavier whenever you try to carry them into a season where they don't belong. Time, talents, and purpose are terrible things to waste. Unapologetically bloom, build, and boss up—with or without others.

Let It Go

You've held on to it long enough: the pain, the sadness, and the hindsight. You replay your downfall like a broken record and keep the words of those who hurt you on repeat. It's not that the journey is beyond difficult. The problem is that you're holding on to the heartbreak, hurt, and humiliation instead of help, hope, and healing.

As hard as it may be, you have to release. Latch on to forgiveness, understanding, and truth. Let go of the regret, hindsight, and the hurt that is weighing you down.

Closure

Holding a grudge only keeps you connected to whatever or whoever caused you pain. Don't seek revenge. Seek release. Let go of it all: the anger, hatred, guilt, shame, resentment and all that is rotting away at your spirit and mind. That is what gives you peace and brings you true closure. It isn't the reaction of someone else. It's your release of the offense.

When you reach the season
you've been praying for,
you will realize why
you had to go through the fire
to get there.

From the Outside Looking In

Whenever you're in the midst of a situation or relationship, your bias and emotions have the tendency to blind you. You are so accustomed to routine that sometimes you fail to see that something is wrong.

For years I struggled with seeing the bigger picture. I tolerated chaos because I was used to it and found myself drowning in anxiety because I simply couldn't handle it. I didn't even know where to begin. It wasn't until I detached that I realized what had been eroding my peace for so long. The same practice applied whenever it came to the journey of healing and self-assessment. I had to distance myself to get a better view of what I didn't want and what I truly needed.

If you are in a season where you are riddled with anxiety, questioning everything, or tired of the trials—I encourage you to take multiple steps back. Embrace isolation and seek to identify the true impact of your environment and thought process. Giving yourself the space and time to analyze your past and present can very well change the course of your health and future.

Press On

Sometimes it's the memories of our past mistakes, pains and problems that make us feel like we aren't good enough to move forward. Other times, it's the opinions of the world that lead us to believe that we will never find our true place in it.

No matter what you feel, just remember that being stuck is just that...a feeling.

You are free to continue the journey without condemnation and insecurity. You are free to let go of the person you once were. Because the only thing in life that keeps you stuck is the belief that you always will be.

The Fork in the Road

Many of us are missing out on growth because we are holding on to people who may have been compatible with our past but are not suitable for our future. Some of us are walking in bitterness, anxiety, and anger because we willingly entertain toxicity that's related to us or has been in our lives for years. Few of us understand that it's our inability to disconnect from dysfunction that's leading to our own destruction.

Before you give another ounce of energy to your burdens, remember it's that very action that is blocking your blessings. Sometimes you have to block access, place boundaries, and ignore others so you can be open to accept blessings, think clearly, and move forward in life.

Moving Forward

Sometimes the hardest yet most rewarding thing we can do in life is silence the noise around us, pick ourselves up, and build the strength to put one foot in front of the other.

It almost seems easier to hold ourselves prisoners to our pasts, view ourselves through a lens dictated by outside validation, or remain stagnant in environments that we realize no longer suit us. Why? Because, quite frankly, that's what we know.

At its core, the ability to wither away in an endless cycle or embark on a journey of accountability, acceptance, and actualization are just the same. They are both choices, energy, and directions we ultimately choose to go.

Focus on who you are and who you are destined to become, instead of worrying about what others think about you and the limits they try to project. This journey is all your own. Never quit moving forward.

God wastes nothing. Every pain, every tear, and every waiting season has a greater purpose. Don't give up. Give it to Him.

The Ride

True friendship and unconditional love are rare because each one requires a level of reciprocity that some are not willing to express.

Not everyone you love, protect, or defend will do the same for you. Sometimes the people you would do anything for will not lift a finger for you. It's a painful yet powerful truth to accept, but sometimes the lesson is less about trusting or expecting things from others and more about the importance of being able to stand by yourself. Being able to clap for yourself. Being able to grow even whenever it seems like everyone and everything is against you.

Not everyone is going to ride with you, but you have to keep going.

To You and Your Journey

To the person who is actively working and trying to become a better version of themselves but is constantly reminded of their past failures and flaws...silence the scrutiny and focus on your goals. To the person who feels like they are losing the support of others as they grow on their journey of mental and spiritual health...remember that pruning is painful but necessary if we want progress. To the person whose own family and friends laugh at their efforts and wait on their demise...remember that God is preparing a table in the presence of your enemies.

Mental and spiritual growth is the toughest fight and most beautiful journey you will ever embark on. Accept the fact that it won't always be accepted or appreciated by everyone else. Understand that you will be the topic of conversation and even put down by people you once lifted up. It's all okay.

It doesn't matter who is against you, as long as God is for you.

Forgive Yourself

It's amazing how quickly and truly we forgive others, yet we are
so slow to extend that level of forgiveness to ourselves.
We carry the inner shame, embarrassment, anger, and regret with
us for so long that we allow that unwillingness to let to go to
become part of us. We must accept the fact that whatever we
did/said or failed to do/say may have been a difficult part of our
journey, but it is not the end. We all fall short, but what's
important is that we get up and move forward with the lessons
we've learned. Let today be the day that you forgive yourself.
You deserve to be free.

The Fight

Ever felt that as you grow mentally and spiritually you struggle in other aspects of your life? Sometimes your friends and family don't seem to understand, you feel alone, and there are distractions everywhere you turn. If it feels like you're in the fight of your life, it's because you are. You're in that transition period between who you once were and who you're striving to be.

There will be challenges, it will get rough, and your faith will be tested. You will question yourself, your direction, and even your progress. But in those times, I encourage you to smile the most. I encourage you to pray the most. I encourage you to research the most. I encourage you to self-assess the most.

In the midst of that personal storm, you have to take refuge in the fact that those are the very times that are going to cause you to blossom the most. So, take every uncomfortable growing pain as validation that you're going the right way. Because one day, you will look back on this very season with laughter, love, and lessons—knowing that everything was used for your good.

Give It to God

You've been carrying the weight long enough. It's time to release and move forward. Give God every worry that is clouding your mind and judgement. Give Him the mistakes of yesterday and condemnation that is keeping you stuck there. Give Him those people who have hurt you to your core. Give Him your past, present, and future. Most importantly, give Him your cares, concerns, tears, and hopes—and then walk away.

Don't let your discomfort or timetable lead you to believe that God doesn't have it handled. He's got it in His way and in His time. Give everything to Him and keep it there. Some battles simply are not ours to fight or figure out.

Embrace Yourself

Why is it that we see the good in everyone but ourselves? We have patience with strangers, lose sleep over people who don't give the slightest care about us, and drop everything to help friends and family yet we always somehow fail to speak life into, believe in, and love ourselves. It's time we give ourselves the encouragement, compassion, and understanding that we give the world. Forgive yourself for not having the wisdom before you learned the lesson. Leave God with that pain/prayer/problem you've been giving and taking out of His hands. Walk in your grace and give glory along the way. You are one of a kind, worthy of the best, and more powerful and important than you give yourself credit for. It's time to accept and act like it.

Emitting the Right Energy

Imagine if you used the energy it takes to hold on to bitterness, unforgiveness, strife with your enemies and regrets and used it to enhance, encourage, and appreciate your loved ones and yourself. Instead of carrying burdens, you would release blessings. Instead of holding grudges, you'd harbor gratefulness.

Be Free

Critics and condemning thoughts will try to keep you in a box that you no longer belong in. Rid yourself of that mindset and misery. It doesn't matter what you've done, who you've been, or how long you lived life going in the wrong direction. You are free to grow and outgrow. You are free to change your routine, mindset, and circle. You are free to try new things that challenge and excite you. This is your life and your story.
Make adjustments as needed.

If it doesn't bring
peace, profits, or purpose
then don't give it
your time, energy, or attention.

Stop following people
who are lost.

I'm far more concerned with
the direction and progression of my life
than the people who approve
or want to come with me.

Lost and Found

Maybe the whole point of getting lost is to purposely find your way back to who you are.

It's difficult. It can feel hopeless to find yourself in a season where nothing seems to be going right and every effort only makes things worse. For every step forward there always manages to be ten steps back. But maybe that's the point of it all. Maybe we are experiencing this level of discomfort because God wants our attention. Maybe He wants us to focus on our mental health and things within, instead of getting wrapped up in the world and everything around us. Maybe He wants us to experience lack so we can truly appreciate the growth and abundance that is coming. Whatever that reason may be, find yourself grateful. Be grateful for the positives you have and the problems that you don't. Give thanks in your progress and focus only on moving forward. This journey has never been or will ever be about anyone else.

People are entitled to
their own opinions.
They are not entitled to
your time, energy, or presence.

Turn the Page

Your journey is your story. You are free to make edits and throw in a plot twist any time that you want. The problem is that you let your negative self-talk or critics narrate your stories. No matter if that chapter was a complete disaster or the most shameful season of your life—you can use those lessons to develop your character, vision, and purpose. Your story is far from over. It's time to turn the page.

You Turn

It is never too late and you are never too old to turn your life, mindset, and self around. The beautiful thing about life is that you are by no means obligated to be the person you were yesterday. So, allow today to be the day you let it all go. Let go of any unforgiveness, regret, shame, or anger that is weighing you down. Boldly and unapologetically take steps in the right direction.

Direction Discernment

Stop expecting people to heal you from a hurt they've never had
or expecting them to give you a better direction for your life
when they can't seem to stay on their own track.

The Answer Is Within You

You already have what it takes to make your dreams a reality. Silence your fears and turn up your focus. The only thing that stands between you and greatness is your ability to take that first step.

For years I hid behind the potential of who I truly could be.
Scared that it would force me to outgrow the people around me
that I knew couldn't or wouldn't want to grow with me.

But still, knowing the risk,
I stopped walking on eggshells
and stepped out of my comfort zone.

Take it one day and one step at a time.
You may not be where you want to be,
but you're closer than you've ever been.

Follow Your Path

It's better to look like a loner who's headed in the right direction compared to being accepted by the crowd and going nowhere at all. Not everyone who gives you advice knows what's truly right for you. Seek discernment and understand that the popular route is not always the progressive one.

Follow the path that is right for you—even if you have to travel alone.

Normal

I wanted nothing more than to go back to normal only to discover that normalcy should be everchanging. To go back would mean regressing to my broken way of living, thinking, and accepting. In turning back, I would be turning away from my self-work. But now, in this foreign season, I see that the discomfort is about the person I am becoming. The past is for an expired version of myself who was comfortable but not conducive to my growth.

The journey will not be easy, but whenever you finally reach that level of peace, progress, and purpose you've been working toward, I promise you will never want to go back.

Love Always

The world is not always nice, but that doesn't mean that we shouldn't strive to be. So often we harden our hearts because at some point or another they were broken. Whether it was due to the ugliness of others or foolishness of ourselves, we learned to protect ourselves by putting up walls or turning off parts of us that brought others light.

There comes a point that we have to let people in. We must have hope, compassion, and faith again. We can't stop doing good because we fear what's bad.

Release to Refine

And you began the journey of letting everything go. Every person, problem, pain, and foolish thought that once held you back became the very basis of what your purpose was: to learn, grow and lead. You see, none of those experiences ever ruined you because they were allowed on your path to refine you.

Sometimes the greatest test
is how you quietly handle those
who so boldly mishandled you.

Red flags and gut feelings are signs.
Don't say God isn't answering
when you refuse to listen.

Growth, healing, and enlightenment do not happen overnight. It takes time, persistence, and the willingness to change. You may not be where you want to be in life but rest assured that each step you've been taking in the right direction is getting you closer to the person you strive to be. Don't fret the length of time. Focus on your level of growth.

You don't need to say you've
been disappointed or disrespected.
You simply need to detach.

Ascension > Acceptance

Don't let loneliness
lead you back
to people and things
God already revealed
and removed.

You can love, pray for,
and bless people
but not want them
to be a part of your life.

That does not
make you mean.
Boundaries without bitterness
are great signs of maturity.

Just because I don't want you
to be a part of my life,
it doesn't mean I want you
to experience pain in yours.

BLOOMING BARE

I can love you
with every ounce of my being
and protect you with a boldness
that can't be ignored,
but I refuse to leave
my heart or life open
to anyone who doesn't value
their place in it.

If you keep trying to hold
someone back with their past,
they won't want to make you a part
of their future.

The Door

You are more than welcome
to walk out of my life,
but do not act surprised
when I close the door behind you.

No matter if their disrespect, betrayal, or toxicity spoke volumes—you have to cut some people off without a sound.

Stop fighting so hard
to hold on to people
who have no fear
of losing you.

I will love you, support you, protect you, and encourage you from the depths of my soul, but I have my limits. Please, don't ever let my empathy or love lead you to believe that I will purposely allow anyone access to my life who will bring toxicity or strain. I cannot and I will not.

Don't let my kindness confuse you.
I will cut you out of my life, if needed.

Sometimes you have to burn bridges
that have the influence to lead you
to destruction, depletion, or depression.

If you have to remind them of your value,
they aren't worth keeping.

Lock for Self-Love

The door to your life, love, and future can't be open to everyone. Sometimes it's your forgiving and empathetic nature that leads others to believe that you will always take them back and let them into your life. Maybe it's the fact that you always looked past problems to keep the peace in your friendships or relationships. But there comes a point that you have to stop choosing people that don't choose you. If you want to grow, you have to detach from what pulls you down. Free yourself from one-sided relationships, wishy-washy friends, and those that take you for granted.

You are worth too much to continuously settle for less.

Hearsay

I used to worry about what you'd say when people asked about me and why I was no longer around. Then I realized that wasn't my concern or problem. My focus was no longer on what people thought about me, but what I felt about myself. What I knew about myself. What I protected within myself. So, say what you want, think what you want, and perceive reality however you want. It's not about your idea of me or even your feelings. It's about the fact that my detachment was for my growth, wellbeing, and health and I was not sacrificing my self-love for anyone who clearly didn't love me.

There is nothing I lost
that I want back

Sometimes the person
you need to forgive most
is yourself

Keep That Energy

When all is said and done, I don't want your apology. I forgave you a long time ago. I don't want to talk about anything, because trust me, enough has already been said. I just want you to keep that same energy, keep that same distance, and keep all of the lessons that you're in alignment to learn.

I forgave you for an apology I was never given
because my closure was never tied
to a single one of your words.
It was dependent upon my willingness to let go.

Detachment stemming from forgiveness is complex yet simple. There is no hatred, grudge, or bitterness because there is no desire for attachment at all.

Let It Be

Today, I release you. The pain associated with every memory, every hope for the future I once had for you, and every limit I placed on myself while waiting for you to become who I hoped you'd be. I forgive and see past the apology you never gave me and see our time as not wasted but as necessary steps toward my wisdom. Today, I release you so I can free myself once and for all.

Chains of Choice

You can't defeat a demon you refuse to detach from, and you can't free yourself from strongholds, toxicity, foolishness, and unnecessary pain if you choose to entertain, engage with, or happily gain attention from them. Healing is a choice and change is uncomfortable, but if you want to be free—you have to learn to let go of what's truly holding you down.

Extend the forgiveness
you so easily give
to others
to yourself.

Grow Without Guilt

You may feel guilty and not everyone will understand, but deep within your heart you will know when a chapter has come to an end. Move forward, seek greatness unapologetically, and remember that there will be growing pains. It's not forgetting where you came from. It's respecting and working toward becoming the person you were created to be.

The Tide is Turning

When the sound of pettiness turned to the sound of crickets, that's when I knew the tide had turned.

Let me tell you an unpopular truth. Whenever you step out on faith or change the direction for your life, you will get commentary. There will be people who are rooting for your growth, supporting you from the beginning, and also trying to genuinely help you in any way that they can. There will also be people who make a joke out of every move you make, pray for your demise, or voice a multitude of reasons as to why you won't succeed.

The beautiful part about each group's efforts is that they have as much power as you give them. In my eyes—I give them both the power to inspire, and I encourage you to do the same.

Remember that no one starts at the very top. The beginning of any endeavor will be filled with trial and error. People will talk, but it doesn't mean that you have to entertain. Embrace the process and allow it to humble your heart and enhance your endurance.

Weak people are always loud
when you're losing
but watch how they whisper
when you win.

BLOOMING BARE

MORGAN RICHARD OLIVIER

Embracing

Irony

Isn't it ironic how as we grow, we simultaneously outgrow?

The things that once enraged us suddenly don't warrant our slightest reaction. The structure, people, music, mindsets, outfits, and influences we once believed we couldn't live without brought the most peace to our lives after we removed them. The way we viewed rejection, happiness, worth, and success shifted after we realized the complexity of protection, joy, and alignment.

You see, our journey is less about finding out who we are. It's about losing the idea and pressure of who we and the world think we ought to be. It's about tackling our toxic traits, uncovering our inner strength, discerning actualization from conditioning, and aligning ourselves with purpose, passion, and spiritual power.

It was never intended for others to understand, because the true beauty always lied in understanding, loving, and accepting ourselves.

Once you realize all that you're worth,
you'll stop tolerating less than you deserve

It's the fact that
you're so unbothered
that bothers them most.

Dripping Joy

There's a joy in my heart that can't be contained and a song in my soul that I can't stop singing. It doesn't come from perfection, people pleasing, or profits. It doesn't come from the opinions of others, outside validation, or anything the world can ever give. My joy drips from the cup of change and the breaking of mental, spiritual, and emotional chains.

I've learned from the challenges of chastising and pressures of pruning. I have grown to honor my journey, love myself fully, and to be still and know that God has not only made a way but always has the final say. All things are working together for my good.

So, excuse the contagious laughter that freedom has given me, and pardon the smile that stems from my readiness for what's to come. This is a brand new season. I'm boldly and gladly walking in it.

Don't let social media confuse you.
You know what I look like.
You do not know who I am.

Your tactics never stopped me.
They gave me endurance.

I lost you but I found myself
and in the depth of my heart
I know that's the very love
I searched for all along.

MORGAN RICHARD OLIVIER

Fix Your Crown

There is no one more determined
than an awakened and empowered queen
reclaiming her throne and taking all
that is rightfully hers.

I Am

I've decided that I am free to be what
and who I was created to be.
I am free to choose a path that honors my progress
and stimulates my growth.
I am free to love, forgive, and embrace all that I truly am.

I am confident, joyful, and grateful.
I am resilient, tried, and true to myself.
I am ready to move forward.

It's time that I put down every burden, regret, and pain—and
boldly walk into my freedom. It doesn't matter who I was
yesterday or who people think I am today. I am walking in my
truth and standing in my authority. I am free to let go and move
forward. My purpose and progress depend on it.

Inner Beauty

The most captivating
form of beauty
is one that is expressed
but not seen—
deeply felt
yet never touched.

Refined and Ready

Don't let past pain or problems keep you from living a life of purpose. We're all a work in progress. Learn your lessons, forgive yourself and others often, and see every experience as an opportunity to grow. You have too powerful of a testimony to let bad memories or emotions hold you back. Speak your truth, share your wisdom, and spread your smile. The world needs what you have. It's time to embrace and express it.

Success

For a very long time, I foolishly believed that success meant wealth or prominence. I thought that it came from overworking, outperforming others, and acquiring an abundance of material things. Thank God I learned that success is anything that you want it to be. My version of success is less about money and more about meaning. To be successful is to be living out my purpose, surrounded by people I love and trust while I grow into the person I was created to be.

Success is being at peace, progressing in various areas of my life, and walking in my obedience and authenticity. It is the ability to look in the mirror and love the person that is looking back. It's the ability to look around me and see joy, love, and a greater meaning of life. Do not let social media, expectations, or your negative self-talk fool you. Sometimes more success simply means less burdens.

Sometimes I look back on my life not to regret but to revel in all that God has done. Every single step of the journey was used for something greater. To say that I am grateful is an understatement. He has definitely made beauty from my ashes.

Walk in Wisdom

Ever look back on life and reminisce on your toughest season?
You know—that time of your life filled with experiences that
hurt you, pushed you, and made you question everything. The
beauty about those ugly chapters is that they typically leave you
with an at times overlooked gift—insight. Instead of focusing on
all that you lost, take a step back and identify all that you gained.
Oftentimes it's that very season that leaves you with endurance,
empathy, strength, wisdom, and a greater understanding of life.
Don't let those memories and times destroy you or your
confidence. Embrace every lesson and allow them to develop
your purpose, vision, and character.

The Puzzle

Even the broken pieces
found a way to fit
ever so beautifully
into this mess of
a masterpiece
we call life.

To the Girl I Once Was

I often find myself thinking about you,
who you once were,
and how your life would be now
if nothing would have ever changed.

And as I see sit here reminiscing about all that has left you, I'm
at peace as I revel in knowing all that remained. You are so
different in the world yet so familiar to the spirit. I find you
dancing on top of the experiences that once brought you
depression and singing about the storms that brought you
struggles and birthed your strength. You amaze me, surprise me,
and act as my motivation daily. Because you may have taken the
long path to get here, but your journey ended up just as beautiful
as your destination.

You don't have to be
a perfect person to be
a powerful one.

Your pain matters.
Your opinion matters.
Your perspective matters.
Do not lose your voice over the lack of outside validation.
The world needs to hear what you have to say.

Lessons Learned

After the dust has settled, time has passed, and overdue lessons have been learned—it all makes sense. Everything that you felt was going to destroy you was used to develop your character, faith, and endurance. You begin to understand the whys of your life and difficult seasons. Most importantly, you find yourself grateful for the perspective you gained in the midst of your storms. So, focus on that. Stop replaying failed scenarios, bad memories, and painful past problems. Look at the lessons. Bask in the blessings that sprang forth from your acquired wisdom. Sing of the strides you've made. All things worked together to make the resilient person that you are today. What was broken is now beautiful.

MORGAN RICHARD OLIVIER

Compete with the person
you were yesterday
instead of comparing
yourself to other people

Don't ever let your inability to identify
and appreciate my value lead you to believe
that I don't know and honor my worth.

The most beautiful thing about her cannot be seen.
It is not found in her measurements
or the clothes that she wears.
It's in the depth of her thoughts,
content of her character,
and the serenity of her soul.

Love yourself to the point that you have zero tolerance
for any disrespect, negative energy, and one-sided relationships.

Push Through

Pray for and envision the person you were born to be, and do not stop until you become that person. It does not matter who accepts your change, who is along for the ride, or even who questions the validity of your transition. Keep pushing through until you make yourself proud.

The time will come
where you will need more,
and when you do
don't settle for less

I realized I was healed when
the new love of myself outweighed
the old hatred I once felt for you.

I learned that the person
whose love I needed to
fight for and protect most
was my own

Do not ever confuse
my love for you
with the willingness
to lose myself.

Phrases like "you know how they are" are no longer acceptable. I don't care if you are a family member, someone I've known for years, or someone I met today. Your disrespect is not acceptable to me simply because it's expected by everyone else.

Disrespect is not disregarded
simply because it's followed
by a compliment

Let Them Lose You

You need to let people lose you
Let them go along with the crowd
Let them believe what they want to believe
Let them think they have better
Let them sleep on your worth

Because in due time
they will realize the mistake they made,
and it will be just enough time for you
to accept that you're better off without them.

There is nothing I enjoy more than
minding my own business,
finding new ways to grow,
and making moves in silence.

You say antisocial.
I say at peace.

She has a fire in her soul
that has the power to warm your heart
or burn your ego to the ground

Never Duplicated

You can imitate my lifestyle
and think you know how it feels
but you'll never have what it takes
to walk a mile in my high heels.

I'm a strong, humble, and talented woman.
My intellect will take you by surprise.
When's the last time you saw a young soul
unapologetically this woke or this wise?

When growth is your constant mindset
and God is gracefully your glue,
you find peace and confidence in knowing
that no one can ever be you.

I'm a Woman

It's not my job to boost your ego or dull my shine
to make you comfortable.
I'm not a puppet that can be controlled
or silenced at your command.
I have the right to express my opinions and emotions,
and it doesn't make me weak or difficult if I choose to do so.

I'm not a princess looking to fit in glass slippers.
I'm a queen who is ready and able to shatter glass ceilings.
Call me what you want but my credentials, talents, and purpose
speak for themselves.

Because I am a fierce and favored woman,
refined by God and walking boldly in His purpose.
I will be who and all that I'm called to be,
and I cannot and will not be stopped.

My intellect is my sexy;
my figure is your distraction.

If only you could see
my beautiful mind.

BLOOMING BARE

No matter how long
or how hard you search,
you will never come close
to finding me in another person.

All of your effort
will never measure up
to my essence.

She is the kind of woman
who will never seek
your approval to be amazing
or lose her peace
to prove a point.

BLOOMING BARE

If you knew how powerful you are,
you'd never second guess
or hold yourself back again.

You can be for me
or rise against me,
but one thing you'll never do
is stand in my way.

Mind your business,
crush your goals,
and make moves in silence.
You don't need an audience
to achieve greatness.

You need to focus.

MORGAN RICHARD OLIVIER

When God has His hand on your life,
it doesn't matter who has your name in their mouth.

Let them be wrong.
There is no need to correct words that will be eaten later.

Allow yourself to be so focused on living in peace, getting paid, and walking in purpose that you have no time to worry about people pleasing, pettiness, or irrelevant opinions.

Rise

I used to think the scariest and most uncomfortable emotion to experience was rejection. Just the thought of being misunderstood, judged, or disliked terrified me. But in time, I grew to realize that being rejected is nothing in comparison to living as an unfulfilled version of myself. I went from fearing peoples' thoughts of me to understanding the importance and power of my own. As I walk into a season of truth and testimony, I'm reminded that I'm far from perfect, yet somehow all of my imperfections work together for my purpose. Remember that it doesn't matter how many flaws you have, how many times you've failed or how the world views you. What's important is that you accept yourself and understand that sometimes rejection is your truest form of protection.

Don't let fear keep you from walking in your truth. Rise and revel in who you've become.

May every kind thing you do
be out of love,
not for love.

Be a Good Person without Persuasion

Be a good person but don't kill yourself trying to prove it. Some people will never like you, will always think you're too much or not enough, and even take your genuine gestures as fake. That is life. Don't let that fact consume your every thought, action, and movement. Keep your intentions pure, always try to do the right thing, and look at every life experience as a tool to help you grow. Another person's disapproval is meaningless if your motives are good.

Embrace Empathy

You don't have to experience hardship, discrimination, or injustice to extend empathy to a community or cause. You simply need compassion and the desire to make a greater change. Learn to love and listen to the concerns, pains and passions of others—even if you don't identify or understand them.

It's Yours

No matter if people question you, condemn you, or misunderstand your ascension—grow and thrive unapologetically. Do not let opportunities pass you by because you don't think others will be comfortable with your success. Do not second guess your talents and abilities because they aren't common or understood by the masses. You have to grow, heal, and thrive for the betterment of yourself. Choose progress over people pleasing and you will excel every time.

Do not look back on life with feelings of regret for the nice things you once did for the wrong people or the wrong things you did with the right intensions. Instead, be grateful for the insight you gained from each of them.

The Comeback

To the person that has been hiding as a result of hindsight and holding yourself back due to fear of rejection—it's time to rise. You've learned your lessons, you've grown, and you're ready to use your endurance and enlightenment for greater things. This is the season where it all makes sense. Where your energy will say it all and the comeback will make the setback worth it. Move in silence if you must, but always remember that you are not walking alone.

I was never made to fit in your box.
I'm here to make you think outside of it.

Don't let the desire to hide in comfort
hinder you from honoring the person
you've become.

The goal is not simply to be new.
It's to be yourself, love yourself, and accept yourself
to the point that no matter who or what life throws at you,
you can lose your way without completely losing who you are.

The Greater Yes in No

Lately, I've been grateful for all of the no's I've received throughout my life and feeling relief where I once felt rejection. My life at 29 is not what I expected and wanted it to be whenever I was 24. In fact, it's better.

In my early twenties, my goals were different. What I wanted for myself was oftentimes an extension of what others expected of me, and the true desires of my heart were at a much smaller scale than what I'm walking in now. I got lost along the way and experienced difficult seasons of what I thought was rejection. But I found two things that changed the course of my life forever: God and my actual self.

Now, since the dust has settled, I recognize and appreciate that God had to allow me to wreck my plans because His was much greater. The opportunities, relationships, and personal growth I have now wouldn't have been possible if He would have answered some of my prayers in the past.

Because of the no's, I'm not the person I thought I wanted to be, and I couldn't be more grateful.

Unapologetic

I can't apologize for not being the person I once was because I don't regret my change at all. Truth is, you're right. I'm not the same. I'm no longer the "I'll always be there for you" type of person. It's not because I don't love you or because I think I'm too good now. It's because I know my worth and have to protect the person I am becoming. I've grown, have boundaries, and I'm serious about my purpose. I can't and won't turn back for anyone. I love you but not enough to hurt myself or sacrifice the peace I now have in my life.

In the review of my destruction
it became clear that I did not lose myself.
I lost the shell of who I was and
who I thought I was supposed to become.

Here I Stand

For such a long time, I struggled to appreciate, understand, and truly value the woman in the mirror.

I easily extended love, gratitude, and patience to every person that crossed my path yet seldom offered an ounce of that goodness to myself. I was blessed but walking with unseen burdens. I was smiling in crowds but struggling in solitude. It took God, grace, and actively pursuing purpose and healing to open my eyes, heart, and mind to who I am and what I am truly here for.

No, I am not perfect. I still make mistakes and find myself learning through trial and error. I am not the fun friend. I am not everyone's favorite person. My body is not without flaw.

However, I love my mind, body, and spirit to a level that was unthought of before. I have purpose, direction, and peace. I rest and create with ease. I see progress and alignment in my life. I know and value the people that I can trust and who truly love me. I embrace all that I am and all that I'm not. I'm a fraction of who I once was, but I'm more whole than I've ever been.

The journey of self-love and healing may not always be the most comfortable, but it is the one that you will never regret taking. Move forward.

Full Circle

Looking back, I see strength that grew in my weakness, joy that stemmed from the lessons of my pain, and a level of awareness that a once naive person never dreamt existed.

That's the thing about looking back on life. We choose what we get out of it. We can have a victim mindset and harp on the problems and pain we experienced, or we can have a growth mindset that shows just how much we've developed along the way.

We will never be perfect people, but I'd rather accept my journey with sincere and purpose filled progress than live condemned and chained to idea of what my journey should have been.

Stepping Stones

Every tear that crossed my face opened my eyes to a greater truth. Every struggle that I thought would take me out strengthened my faith and showed me that I can handle more than I ever knew. Every delay redirected my mindset. Every consequence developed my character. It was the seasons where everything went wrong that got my attention and made me take the steps of getting my mind, spirit, and life right. Every single step of my journey led me to where I am today.

From the brokenness
blossomed a profound beauty.
Powerful with a purpose
for all of life's pain.

BLOOMING BARE

Acknowledgments

To the person that has welcomed my words,
I thank you for not only embracing my journey
but also embarking on your own.

I thank you for meeting my experiences with empathy
and accepting my lessons with love.

May you never forget that healing, happiness, and wholeness
are not found by running to the outside world.
They are developed by returning to the stillness within
your most authentic self.

BLOOMING BARE

About the Author

Morgan Richard Olivier is an American author, advocate, wife, and speaker. With a passion for writing that serves as a form of therapy for both herself and her audience—Morgan's outlet for expression fosters and supports conversations that are needed to stop stigmas and support healing, self-acceptance, and personal growth. Since publishing her first book *Questions, Christ, and the Quarter-Life Crisis* in 2020, Morgan has become a source of encouragement and empowerment to men and women worldwide.

Through empathy and wisdom from lessons learned, she enlightens and inspires others to find the greater purpose in life's pains and pressures. Morgan's goal is to crush the image and pursuit of perfection by captivating the raw beauty of sincere progress.

BLOOMING BARE

INSTAGRAM   **FACEBOOK**   **TWITTER**

@modernmorgan   @modernmorgan   @themodernmorgan

BLOOMING BARE

MORGAN RICHARD OLIVIER

BLOOMING BARE

www.modernmorgan.com

ISBN: 978-1-7359906-4-4

Editor: Dr. Joanna Davis-McElligatt
Cover Illustration by Asher Berard
Interior Design by Lance Butler
Author Photo by Lori Lyman